TALES OF THE DEAD

# ANCIENT CHINA

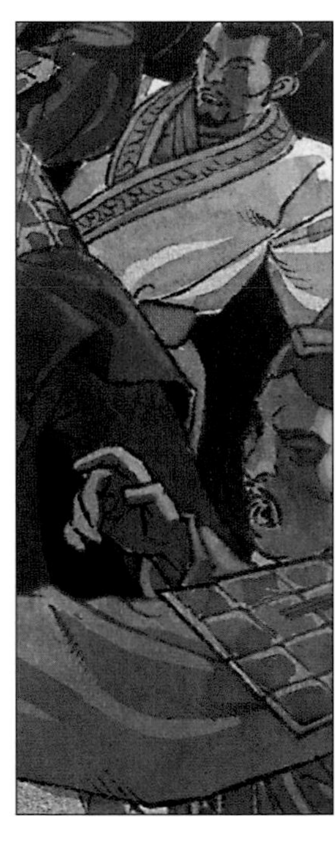
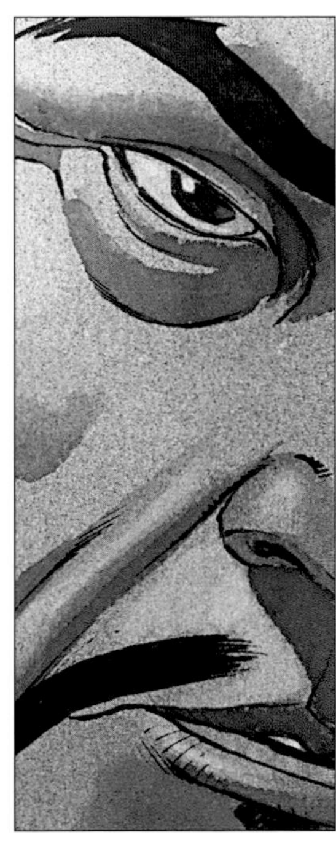

*Written by* Stewart Ross

*Consultant* Mary Ginsberg

*Illustrated by* Inklink & Richard Bonson

LONDON, NEW YORK, MUNICH,
MELBOURNE, and DELHI

**EDITOR** Kate Simkins
**ART EDITOR/STORY VISUALIZER** John Kelly
**DESIGNER** Ron Stobbart
**RESEARCHER/INDEXER** Julia March
**DESIGN MANAGER** Lisa Lanzarini
**PUBLISHING MANAGER** Simon Beecroft
**PUBLISHER** Alex Allan
**PRODUCTION** Amy Bennett
**DTP DESIGNER** Hanna Ländin

First American Edition, 2006
06 07 08 09 10 10 9 8 7 6 5 4 3 2

Published in the United States by
DK Publishing, Inc.
375 Hudson Street, New York, New York 10014



A catalog record for this book is available from the Library of Congress.

ISBN 13: 978-0-7566-2076-7
ISBN 10: 0-7566-2076-9

Color reproduction by Media Development and Printing Ltd., UK
Printed and bound by Leo Paper Products, China

Discover more at
www.dk.com

## ACKNOWLEDGMENTS

Richard Bonson painted the Great Wall (pages 8–9), the junk (pages 14–15), the city (pages 20–21), the terra-cotta army (pages 24–25), and the palace (pages 28–29).

Inklink painted all other artworks, including the graphic novel.

The publisher would like to thank Corbis/Mike McQueen for kind permission to reproduce their photograph on page 4, top left.

# Contents

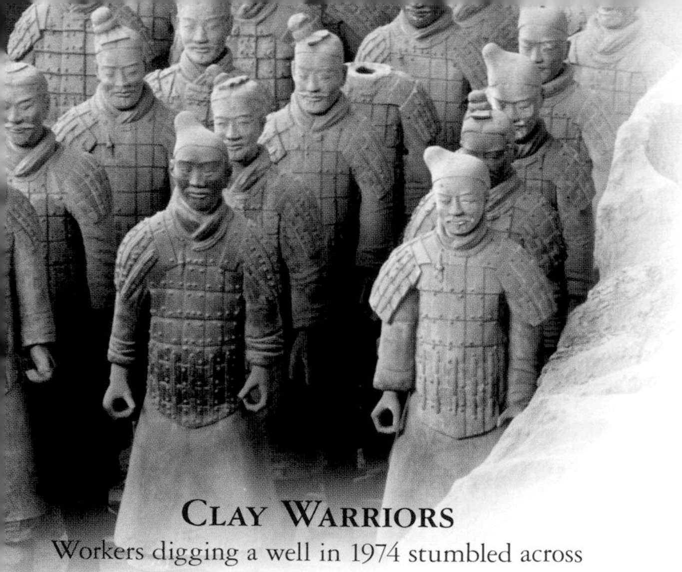

**Clay Warriors**

Workers digging a well in 1974 stumbled across one of the most amazing archeological finds of all time. It was a model army—life-size and many thousands strong—made more than 2,000 years ago to guard the first emperor's tomb.

# An Ancient Land

Ancient China was one of the most amazing civilizations in history. From its beginning, around 5,000 years ago, in small farming villages, China became the greatest empire in the world. Its empire lasted longer than any other—2,000 years—and was also the largest and most advanced the world had ever seen.

Under the empire, education was highly prized and the arts, especially music and painting, flourished. Sciences—including the invention of cast iron and gunpowder—were centuries ahead of the rest of the world. Small wonder the Chinese believed that their emperors ruled with the blessing of heaven.

## Meet the Characters...

**Shen**

"Since I was a young boy, I have been learning to play the zither. I love playing this beautiful stringed instrument and practice every day of my life. Now I am 11, my teachers say I am ready to perform in public. I can't wait to show what I can do."

**Count Gao**

"Most people talk too much. In these difficult times, when traitors and murderers lurk around every corner, it is best to keep your mouth shut. That is my way. It means that no one even guesses what I am up to."

**Meiling**

"I am the daughter of the captain of the guard and the emperor's favorite. I am extremely important and clever. I try to help the emperor by keeping watch over dangerous strangers that enter the royal palace."

Timeline

1969 *Men land on the Moon*

1644 *Ming dynasty ends in China*

1279 *Mongols establish Yuan dynasty in China*

618 *Tang dynasty begins in China*

410 *Roman Empire collapsing*

221 *Qin Empire unites China*

Present Day

2000 CE (COMMON ERA) — 1000 CE — CE (COMMON ERA) 0 BCE (BEFORE COMMON ERA)

Story continues on next page

## Instruments of Death

China, 214 BCE. Qin Shihuangdi, the first emperor, has been ruling the empire for eight years. He is a ruthless leader who has many enemies and lives in fear of assassination. The emperor is able to relax only when soothed by sweet music. As you read Shen's exciting story, discover what life was like in Ancient China.

I AM SHEN...

...A MUSICIAN.

PEOPLE SAID I HAD GREAT TALENT.

### Qin Shihuangdi

"Heaven called upon me to become emperor of all China, and I obeyed its command. Since then I have worked tirelessly to bring law and order to my land. I am troubled, though, because a few evil men are jealous of my power..."

### Duke Song

"We noblemen are proud to serve our mighty ruler Qin Shihuangdi, who united all China and brought us peace. As part of his loyal court, I travel with His Majesty and seek to protect him from his enemies."

## The Middle Kingdom

The Chinese called their land the Middle Kingdom because they believed China was the center of the world. China stretches across central and eastern Asia. It is surrounded by mountains, deserts, and seas. Qin Shihuangdi united the kingdoms of eastern China and built a capital city at Xianyang near present-day Xian. Over the centuries, the empire expanded into central and southern Asia, but its borders changed as lands were won or lost.

North America
Europe
Africa
South America

MONGOLIA
Gobi Desert
Beijing
CHINA
Plateau of Tibet
Xian
Nanjing
Shanghai
HIMALAYAS
Guangzhou
TAIWAN
Bay of Bengal
South China Sea

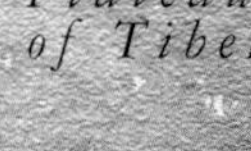

753
*City of Rome founded*

c.1050
*Zhou dynasty starts in China*

c.1400
*Civilization develops on mainland Greece*

c. 2000
*Minoan civilization develops on Crete*

c. 2500
*Indus Valley civilization flourishes in Pakistan*

c. 3100
*Ancient Egypt united*

1000 BCE 2000 BCE 3000 BCE (BEFORE COMMON ERA)

Continued from previous page

# The Greatest Empire

Qin Shihuangdi was China's first emperor. The empire that he set up lasted more than 2,000 years (221 BCE–1912 CE). The emperors who ruled during this time came from different families, known as "dynasties." The first emperor's dynasty, the Qin, took its name from the kingdom that he ruled from the age of 13. "Qin" is pronounced "chin" and it is from this that we get the name "China."

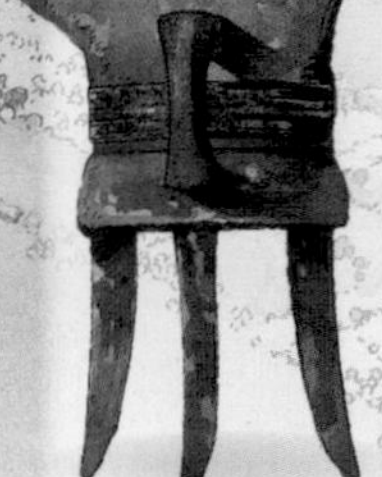
Bronze drinking cup from the Shang period

## Shang c.1500–c.1050 BCE

The Shang dynasty is the earliest period of Chinese history about which there is lots of evidence. At this time, China was divided into several kingdoms. The Shang kingdom in the north was the most powerful. During this time, picture-writing developed, bronze was made into vessels for religious ceremonies, and silk was produced.

Bodyguard watching for assassins

Qin Shihuangdi, the first emperor

Imperial headgear

Special bronze water vessel from the Zhou kingdom

## Western Zhou c.1050–771 BCE

The Zhou dynasty in western China overthrew the Shang and became the most powerful in China. Many smaller kingdoms continued to exist but were ruled by the Zhou, who had their capital city near Xian. Iron, plows, crossbows, coins, and chopsticks were all used for the first time in this period.

## Eastern Zhou 771–221 BCE

In 771 BCE, the Zhou moved their capital city to the east as their power over the other kingdoms lessened. From 475 to 221 BCE, these kingdoms, including the Qin and the Chu, struggled for mastery over China. During this time, known as the Warring States period, great armies fought each other in battles where thousands were killed.

Deadly bronze spearheads

## Qin 221–206 BCE

The ruler of the Qin kingdom defeated the other kingdoms, united China, and founded the empire. He took the name Qin Shihuangdi, which means First Qin Emperor, and began a program of building that included the Great Wall and a magnificent tomb.

Model horse from Qin Shihuangdi's tomb

Groveling nobles

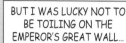

MY TEACHERS MADE ME PRACTICE HARD.
BUT I WAS LUCKY NOT TO BE TOILING ON THE EMPEROR'S GREAT WALL...
FASTER, YOU DOGS!

...LIKE OTHERS IN MY VILLAGE.
I HEARD TERRIBLE STORIES...

...OF DEADLY ACCIDENTS.

THIS ONE'S GONE.
OH, NO! ON YOUR KNEES!


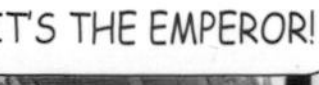

IT'S THE EMPEROR!
QIN SHIHUANGDI...


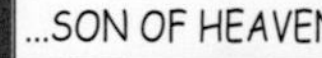

...SON OF HEAVEN...

...LORD OF LIFE...

## Han 206 BCE–220 CE

The Han dynasty lasted longer than any other. It became so respected that the Chinese word for a Chinese person means "a man of Han." The Han emperors started the civil service that ran the country for the next 2,000 years.

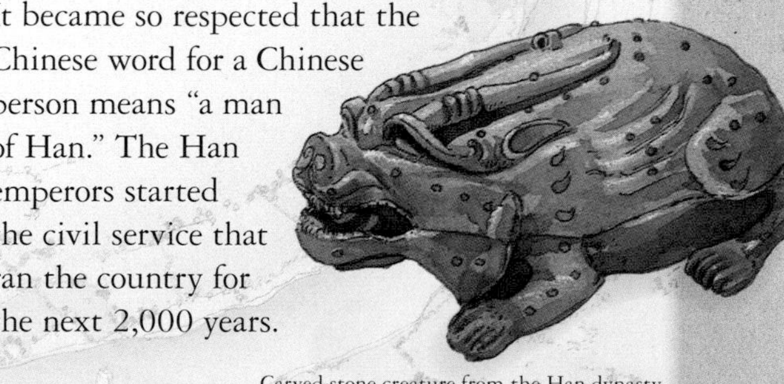

Carved stone creature from the Han dynasty

## Disunity 220–589 and Sui 589–618

For more than 350 years after the fall of the Han, the empire was broken up. At first, it was divided between competing kingdoms. Then, the north and the south were separate empires. The Buddhist religion began to spread during these years. In 589, a general from the north, Yang Jian, reunited the country, founding the Sui dynasty.

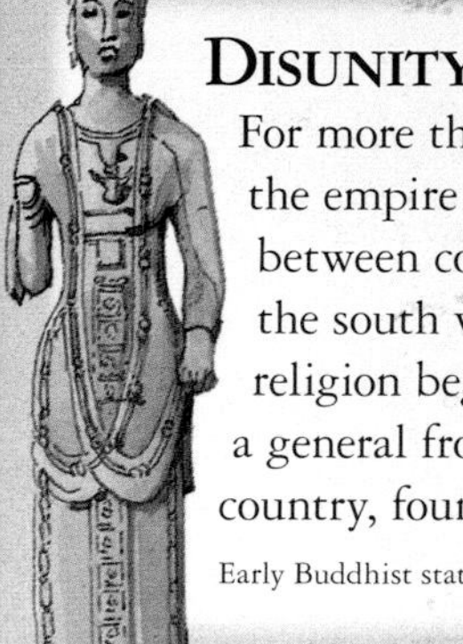

Early Buddhist statue

## Tang 618–907

During the Tang dynasty, the empire expanded and became rich. Able rulers, including Taizong and the only empress, Wu Zetian, continued the civil service system that gave power to the most talented. At the same time, music, dance, poetry, painting, sculpture, and pottery were at their most brilliant.

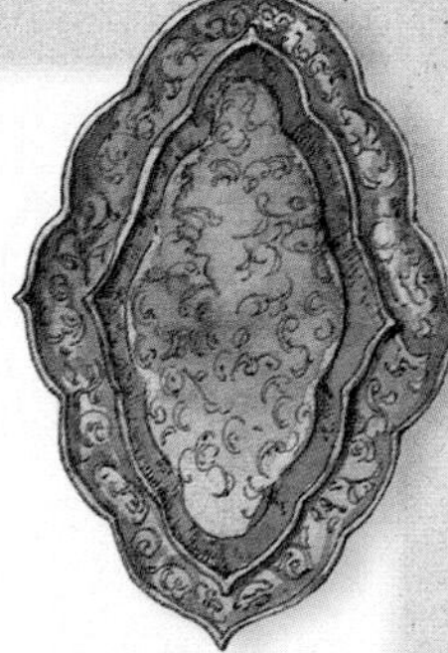

Silver dish from the Tang dynasty

## Song 960–1279

After the collapse of the Tang, China was divided for a time. Then, in 960, the Song reunited the empire. Eventually, they lost control of the north and for about 150 years ruled only in the south. Even so, China flourished under their wise government. There were great advances in science and the arts.

Ceramic ewer from the Song dynasty

## Yuan 1279–1368

In 1215, the Mongol leader Genghis Khan made northern China part of an empire that stretched all the way to Europe. His grandson Kublai Khan seized southern China and established the Yuan dynasty. The Mongols were harsh rulers and were overthrown in a series of rebellions.

Yuan vase

## Ming 1368–1644 and Qing 1644–1912

The Ming dynasty was a time of wealth and stability in which Chinese culture flourished. It was the last Chinese dynasty. The Qing dynasty was ruled by the Manchu, foreigners from the northeast who had adopted Chinese ways. The latter part of their rule was plagued by wars with foreign powers and popular uprisings. Eventually, the people revolted against the Manchu and formed a republic.

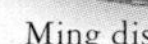

Ming dish

This map shows the extent of the first empire, the Qin, and the last empire, the Qing.

HE'S COME TO DEAL WITH THE CORRUPT OVERSEERS!

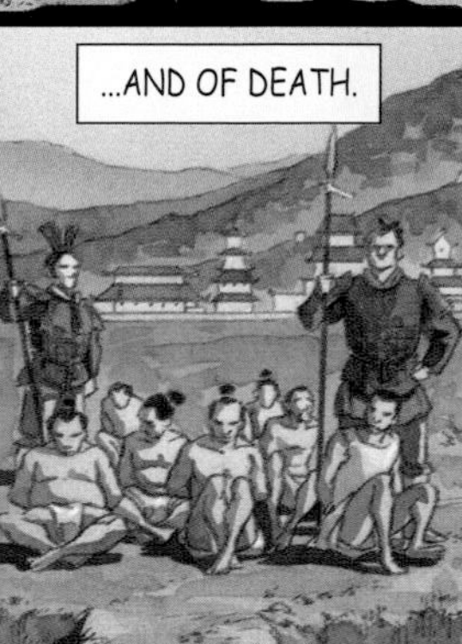
...AND OF DEATH.

NOW HIS HIGHNESS IS PRESENT...
...LET THE EXECUTIONS BEGIN!

THE EMPEROR SAW ENEMIES EVERYWHERE...

...AND DESTROYED THEM...
...UTTERLY.

BUT HE DID NOT REST EASY AT NIGHT...

...UNLESS LULLED BY HIS ZITHER PLAYER'S SWEET MUSIC.

AS THE SOUNDS WASHED OVER HIM...

...HIS TROUBLES SLIPPED AWAY...

...AND HE COULD FINALLY RELAX.

Story continues on next page

Continued from previous page

# The Great Wall

The Great Wall of China was built and rebuilt over many centuries and once stretched about 4,000 miles (6,500 km). Its earliest sections, dating from the fourth century BCE, were put up by the warring states. Under Qin Shihuangdi, the pieces were joined together to protect the empire from invaders from the north. Much of the wall we see today was rebuilt in the Ming dynasty.

THE EMPEROR WAS IN CONSTANT DANGER...
...FROM ASSASSINS.

ANOTHER TUNE, O LORD...
THWACK!

...AARGHH!

GUARDS!
NO ONE NEAR THE EMPEROR WAS SAFE.

### 1 Battlements

The battlements of the Ming wall are made from bricks. There are gaps through which soldiers shoot their crossbows at enemies.

### 10 Smooth Top

Massive bricks weighing about 22 lbs (10 kg) are laid along the top of the wall to make a smooth surface.

### 9 Main Road

The wall is about 19 feet (6 meters) wide at the top. It acts as a road along which five horses can travel side by side.

### 8 Rough Filling

Earth, stones, sand, and even twigs are used to fill the core of the wall. All the material has to be carried into place in baskets.

### 7 Local Materials

The wall crosses farmland, desert, and mountains. It is built with whatever materials are near at hand, even wood and pebbles. Bricks are made from mud nearby.

CAPTAIN! GUARDS!
WHERE ARE YOU?

HERE!
YOUR MAJESTY!
ARGHH!
HE'S ON THE OTHER ROOF!

Story continues on next page
2 Watchtowers
Guards watch for invaders from towers built at intervals along the wall. They signal from tower to tower using fire, flags, and drums.
3 Great Barrier
Most of the wall stands about 25 feet (7 meters) tall. Some Ming sections are faced with stone.
4 Built on High
In mountainous areas, the wall is built on steep slopes that add to the height of the wall, making it even harder to cross.
5 Dangerous Work
Accidents on the wall cost the lives of countless thousands of workers, many of whom are forced to work there as a punishment.
6 Bamboo Support
The workers build scaffolding made of bamboo, which is incredibly strong but flexible. Bamboo is a type of grass that can grow more than 100 feet (30 meters) tall.
The Qin Wall
When he was emperor of all China, Qin Shihuangdi destroyed all walls except those guarding his northwest frontier. He then ordered these to be joined up in the "10,000 Li Long Wall" (1 li equaled 580 yards or 500 meters) that took 10 years to build.
Layers of reeds and clay mixed with pebbles
Heavenly field—a soft trench that shows the footprints of trespassers
Mud bricks
Desert
Many of the workers are criminals
WE'VE GOT HIM CORNERED!
UGH!
GET HIM!
WE COULD NOT TAKE THE ASSASSIN ALIVE.
YOUR MAJESTY, IS IT SAFE FOR YOU TO STAY HERE?
MMM...THE ARROW THAT GOT MY MUSICIAN...
...WAS MEANT FOR ME.
THE COURT WILL RETURN TO THE CAPITAL...
...IMMEDIATELY!
FASTER!
...BY THIS TIME TOMORROW!
BRING ME A NEW ZITHER PLAYER...
AND ONE MORE THING!

Continued from previous page

# Food for the People

Throughout history, the great majority of Chinese dwelled in villages and made their living from farming. The best farmland was around the Huang He (Yellow) and Chang Jiang (Yangzi) rivers and on the Great Plain between them. Millet was the main crop in the dry, cool north, while rice grew well in the warm, wet south. All over the country, village life followed the same pattern of plowing, planting, and harvesting year after year, century after century.

THEY CAME FOR ME IN THE NIGHT.
OPEN UP!
IN THE NAME OF THE EMPEROR!
WHY US? WHAT HAVE WE DONE?
MY PARENTS FEARED THE WORST.
WE'RE TAKING THE BOY!
BUT HE'S DONE NOTHING WRONG!
BE QUIET AND YOU WON'T BE HARMED.
THEY ORDERED ME TO BRING MY ZITHER.
SAVE YOUR TEARS! THE BOY IS WANTED AT COURT.
THEN WE WERE GONE...
...LEAVING MY PARENTS WITH MONEY...
...IN PLACE OF A SON.
River provides fish, as well as water for drinking and irrigation
Digging terraces on steep slopes allows more land to be farmed
Women and men work in the fields
Peasant houses are small and timber-framed with a roof of thatch or tiles
Rice is grown in flooded, muddy fields called paddies

## Grain of Life

Most Chinese ate rice. It tasted good, was easy to cook, provided lots of energy, and was simple to store. Fields produced two or even three crops a year.

## Simple Eating

The diet of the ordinary peasant varied little. It mostly consisted of grain, such as millet, wheat, or rice, eaten with soy and vegetables. Fish was more common than meat.

STORY CONTINUES ON NEXT PAGE

## MOVING WATER

Rice needs to grow in water. By the Song dynasty, new methods of irrigation (watering crops) enabled more fields to be flooded for rice growing. The shaduf allowed water buckets to be easily lifted using a pole counterbalanced with a weight. A paddle pump, driven by peasant leg-power, was a far quicker way of moving large quantities of water.

Water pump driven by peasants who push pedals with their feet

Shaduf for raising water from a lower to a higher level

Weight

Cog-wheel turned by pedals pulls the chain of wooden paddles

Bucket

A chain of wooden paddles pulls water up from the river

River or canal

## FEASTING

A rich man's banquet might have 10 separate dishes. There was rice, of course, but also meat (especially pork), fish, poultry, soup, vegetables, and wine to drink.

## FARMERS

Rice-growing was hard work since shoots were usually grown in nurseries and had to be moved to the flooded paddy field by hand. The wealthy owned most of the land and ordinary people—peasant farmers—had to pay rent for it. With taxes to pay as well, life was tough.

Wooden yoke allows heavy loads to be carried comfortably

Oxen are valuable animals used to pull plows

...AND TO MY AMAZEMENT...

...THE LORD OF THE WORLD SMILED!

TERRIFIED...

...I DID AS I WAS TOLD...

PLAY, CHILD!

THEY SAY THE BOY HAS TALENT, SIRE.

SO BEGAN MY NEW LIFE.
I WAS TAKEN UNDER HEAVY GUARD...
...ANXIOUS NOT TO DO ANYTHING WRONG...
...THOROUGHLY SEARCHED...
...AND LED TO...
...THE EMPEROR!

Continued from previous page

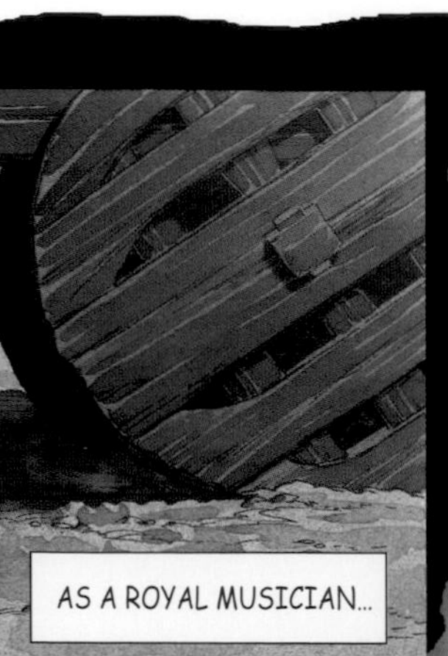
AS A ROYAL MUSICIAN...

...I TRAVELED WITH THE COURT...

...EXAMINING MY NEW COMPANIONS ON THE WAY.

# Chinese Arts

The Chinese had great respect for art and artists. Every educated person was expected to be skilled at calligraphy (beautiful writing), poetry, and painting, and music was an important part of life. The Chinese were skilled craftsworkers, making objects from materials like porcelain, bronze, jade, and silk.

**Oracle Writing**
Chinese writing developed from symbol-pictures like these on tortoiseshell.

**Jade Buffalo**
Jade was a favorite gemstone of the Chinese. It is hard as steel and extremely difficult to work. The Chinese believed it had magical properties.

## Written Chinese

Chinese writing is not based on the sound of the spoken word but on what each character represents. Over thousands of years, the characters changed as new writing tools were used, paper was invented, and people simplified the writing.

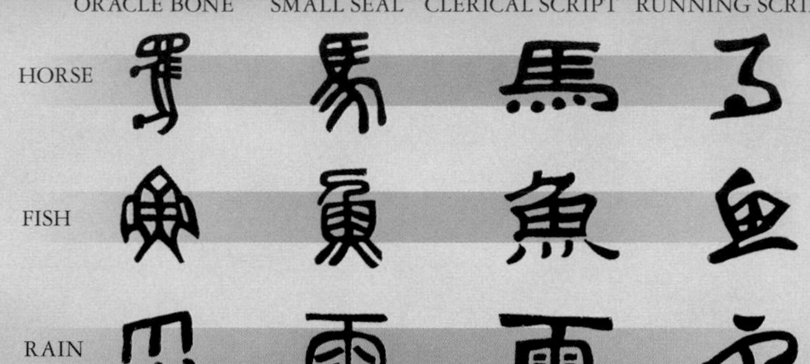
ORACLE BONE
SMALL SEAL
CLERICAL SCRIPT
RUNNING SCRIPT
HORSE
FISH
RAIN

There were many stages in the evolution of Chinese characters—this illustration shows four of them. Early Chinese picture-writing has been found on oracle bones. Small seal script is an old form of writing in use during the Qin dynasty when the emperor unified the language. Clerical script developed as a simpler form of writing for official documents. Running script is a fast, flowing form of writing, often used in calligraphy.

## Learning Calligraphy

Chinese calligraphy was an art form, and calligraphers were highly respected. A scholar needed patience and years of practice in calligraphy to learn the 6,000–8,000 characters he needed. Study was based on copying the handiwork of ancient masters.

Fine brush for writing characters
Inkstone—ink sticks were ground with water on the inkstone
Ink stick made from soot and gum
Ceramic brush rest

**Brilliant Character**
This character, which means "brilliant," is from a poem written in the Song dynasty. The calligrapher used careful strokes of his brush to create an elegant piece of art in his own particular style.

I KNOW WHAT YOU'RE THINKING!
HE'S GAO, COUNT GAO.

LOOKS SINISTER, DOESN'T HE?

I'M DUKE SONG...
...AND YOU MUST BE THE NEW COURT MUSICIAN?
YES, SIR.

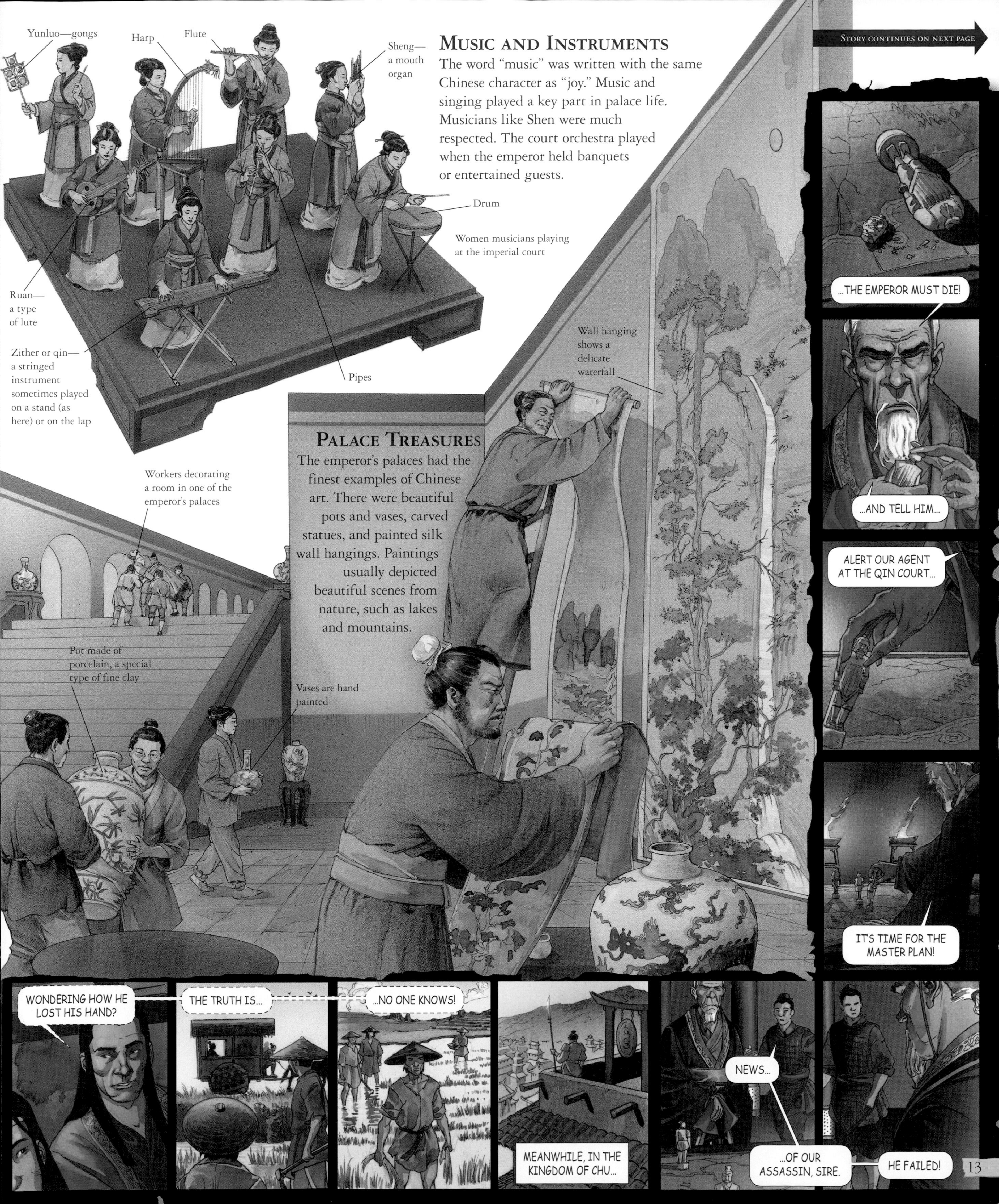

Yunluo—gongs
Harp
Flute
Sheng—a mouth organ
Drum
Women musicians playing at the imperial court
Ruan—a type of lute
Zither or qin—a stringed instrument sometimes played on a stand (as here) or on the lap
Pipes
Wall hanging shows a delicate waterfall
Workers decorating a room in one of the emperor's palaces
Pot made of porcelain, a special type of fine clay
Vases are hand painted
STORY CONTINUES ON NEXT PAGE
WONDERING HOW HE LOST HIS HAND?
THE TRUTH IS...
...NO ONE KNOWS!
MEANWHILE, IN THE KINGDOM OF CHU...
NEWS...
...OF OUR ASSASSIN, SIRE.
HE FAILED!
IT'S TIME FOR THE MASTER PLAN!
ALERT OUR AGENT AT THE QIN COURT...
...AND TELL HIM...
...THE EMPEROR MUST DIE!


## Music and Instruments

The word "music" was written with the same Chinese character as "joy." Music and singing played a key part in palace life. Musicians like Shen were much respected. The court orchestra played when the emperor held banquets or entertained guests.

## Palace Treasures

The emperor's palaces had the finest examples of Chinese art. There were beautiful pots and vases, carved statues, and painted silk wall hangings. Paintings usually depicted beautiful scenes from nature, such as lakes and mountains.

Continued from previous page

# A Chinese Junk

Boats were always an important way of getting around in China. Wooden sailing ships, called junks, were used by merchants to carry goods along rivers and canals or by sea. They were also used by the pirates who stole from them. For many years, Chinese ships were the most advanced in the world. They were the first to have rudders, which allowed large ships to be steered easily.

AT THE NEAREST PORT...
...WE TOOK RIVER JUNKS.
THE EMPEROR WENT ABOARD THE LARGEST BOAT...
...WITH HIS BODYGUARDS...

**1 High Bow**
The bow (at the front) and the stern (at the back) are built up high to prevent the ship from being swamped by water in heavy seas.

**9 Unsinkable**
Unlike ships of other countries, the inside of the junk is divided into watertight compartments. This makes it almost impossible to sink.

**8 Floating Home**
Much of China's inland trade is carried along rivers and canals in vessels like this. It is a floating home as well as a cargo carrier.

**7 Strong Vessel**
Three layers of wooden planks below the water level make the junk strong enough to go to sea.

...AND SET SAIL IMMEDIATELY.

WE FOLLOWED IN A SMALLER VESSEL.
THE MYSTERIOUS COUNT GAO STOOD ALONE.
WHAT'S HE DOING?

AS THE EMPEROR'S JUNK ...
...DISAPPEARED AROUND A BEND IN THE RIVER, DUKE SONG EXPLAINED.

GAO IS A MASTER SWORDSMAN...

STORY CONTINUES ON NEXT PAGE

2 STRONG SAILS
The square or rectangular sails are made of canvas, silk, or matting. Bamboo strips make the sails stiffer and easier to roll up.
3 TALL MASTS
The junk's many masts—the biggest ships have nine—hold the sails and are made from tall, flexible pine trees. Each sail can be positioned differently, allowing the junk to sail almost into the wind.
4 CAPTAIN'S QUARTERS
The captain, his wife, and their children live in their own quarters at the stern. The crew usually sleeps in the hold with the cargo.
5 RUDDER POWER
The rudder is a large, heavy board attached to the stern used to steer a straight course. It is lowered for sailing in deep water.
6 BULK CARRIER
The holds are used to carry goods, such as grain or pottery. The larger junks can store up to 660 tons (600 metric tons) of cargo.
...THE SOLDIERS HAVE ASKED HIM...
...TO SHOW THEM A FEW TRICKS.
FOR WHAT SEEMED LIKE AGES GAO STOOD STILL.
...THEN HIS SWORD SEEMED TO DANCE IN THE AIR...
...AS HIS BLADE FLASHED IN THE SUNLIGHT...
...LIKE SUMMER LIGHTNING.
PIRATES!!!
SOUND THE ALARM!
SMALL BOATS SPED TOWARD US!
SUDDENLY THE BANK WAS ALIVE WITH PEOPLE!

Continued from previous page

THE GUARDS BARKED THEIR ORDERS.

QUICK! BEFORE THEY SEE WE'RE SOLDIERS...
...EVERYONE DOWN!

YOU TOO, SHEN!
HORRIFIED, I WATCHED...

...AS THE PIRATES CAME ON BOARD.

# Governing the Empire

The Chinese emperors adopted the dragon as their symbol. Although it looked fierce, the mythical beast was thought to be wise, strong, and good. The dragon also represented life-giving water.

The Chinese Empire lasted for so long because of its remarkable system of government. Until modern times, nothing else like it existed anywhere else in the world. It was based on three things: an all-powerful emperor; efficient laws with punishment for wrong-doers; and, most important, a civil service made up of people appointed by the emperor to run the empire.

A gold plaque that may have been worn by a minister or prince in late imperial times to show his high rank.

## Harsh Leader

Qin Shihuangdi was the first all-powerful emperor. He was a harsh ruler who controlled his subjects by making strict laws and brutally punishing anyone who disobeyed them. As the first emperor, he forced the nobles from the kingdoms defeated by the Qin to move to his court so he could stop them from plotting against him. In spite of this, there were several attempts to kill him and he lived in fear of his life.

## Terrible Punishment

Each dynasty issued a new law code that set out laws and punishments. Under Qin Shihuangdi, punishments were very severe, including burying alive, beheading, beating, and branding. Torture was also allowed.

## Confucian Ideas

Kong Fuzi (551–479 BCE), known as Confucius, was a great thinker whose ideas greatly influenced Chinese society. He believed in kindness, respect for others, and the importance of the family. When Confucian scholars disapproved of Qin Shihuangdi's harsh rule, the emperor ordered Confucian books to be burned and punished the scholars.

Wooden yoke called a cangue controls the prisoners
Qin guards arrest Confucian scholars

SHHHHHH!

WAIT FOR IT!
ONE...
TWO...

LOOKS LIKE THEY'VE ABANDONED SHIP!

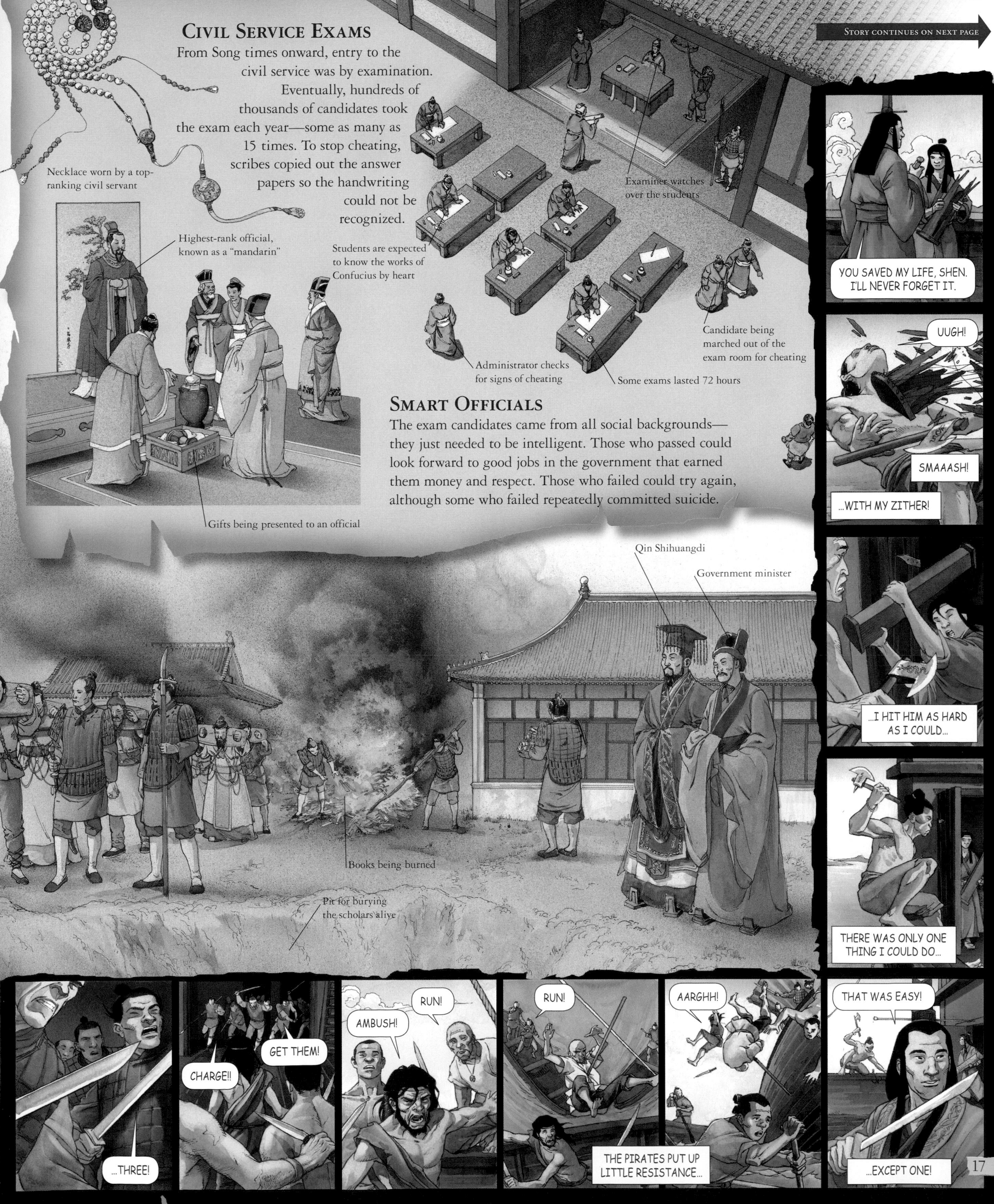

## Civil Service Exams

From Song times onward, entry to the civil service was by examination. Eventually, hundreds of thousands of candidates took the exam each year—some as many as 15 times. To stop cheating, scribes copied out the answer papers so the handwriting could not be recognized.


Necklace worn by a top-ranking civil servant
Highest-rank official, known as a "mandarin"
Gifts being presented to an official
Students are expected to know the works of Confucius by heart
Examiner watches over the students
Candidate being marched out of the exam room for cheating
Administrator checks for signs of cheating
Some exams lasted 72 hours


## Smart Officials

The exam candidates came from all social backgrounds—they just needed to be intelligent. Those who passed could look forward to good jobs in the government that earned them money and respect. Those who failed could try again, although some who failed repeatedly committed suicide.


Qin Shihuangdi
Government minister
Books being burned
Pit for burying the scholars alive
...THREE!
CHARGE!!
GET THEM!
AMBUSH!
RUN!
RUN!
THE PIRATES PUT UP LITTLE RESISTANCE...
AARGHH!
THAT WAS EASY!
...EXCEPT ONE!
THERE WAS ONLY ONE THING I COULD DO...
...I HIT HIM AS HARD AS I COULD...
UUGH!
SMAAASH!
...WITH MY ZITHER!
YOU SAVED MY LIFE, SHEN. I'LL NEVER FORGET IT.


Story continues on next page

CONTINUED FROM PREVIOUS PAGE

# CHINESE TRADE

The Chinese had always traded goods among themselves. Trade with foreigners began during the Han dynasty, when the Chinese discovered the fast horses to the west of their borders and traded silk for them. Soon, a whole network of trade routes was bringing goods, as well as ideas, in and out of China.

## MAKING SILK

Silk is made from the threads of silkworms. About 4,400 silkworms are needed to produce just 2 pounds (1 kilogram) of silk. For thousands of years, the Chinese kept how they made silk a secret. The Romans believed it was made from leaves and their name for China was Serica, the "Land of Silk."

## PAYING WITH MONEY

Before the empire, Chinese coins were different shapes and could only be used in the kingdom where they were made. Some were like miniature knives and spades. The first emperor introduced bronze coins that could be used throughout the Empire. Paper money was invented in China in the 11th century.

## TRANSPORTATION IN CHINA

Heavy goods like grain and fragile goods like pottery were moved by boat. Horses were the favored means of transportation on land, either ridden singly or pulling a cart or coach. They were expensive, however, and an ox cart was the much cheaper alternative used by most ordinary people.

AFTER THE PIRATE ATTACK...
...WE SOON CAUGHT UP WITH THE ROYAL JUNK.
AS WE DISEMBARKED AT THE PORT...
...THE STORY OF WHAT I'D DONE...
...SPREAD QUICKLY.
ONLY COUNT GAO SEEMED UNIMPRESSED.
Knife-shaped coin
Spade-shaped coin
Early bronze coins
Workers pick mulberry leaves to feed to silkworms
Silkworm moth lays eggs that grow into caterpillars called silkworms
Several threads are twisted together to make one strong thread, which is woven into cloth on a loom
Silkworms feed on mulberry leaves
Silkworm spins silk threads to make a cocoon, inside of which it turns into a moth
Mediterranean Sea
Customs house where officials collect tax due to the Emperor
Goods ready to be loaded on a boat
Nobleman's two-horse carriage
Lady's sedan chair
WHAT A HERO, SAVING DUKE SONG!
LEAVE HIM ALONE, GAO!
I OWE HIM MY LIFE!
COME HERE, BOY!
YOUR MAJESTY!!!
WELL, WELL...
...A WARRIOR MUSICIAN! MOST UNUSUAL!

Story continues on next page

IN
OUT
Jade
Horses
Gold
Dyes
Ceramics
Gems
Lacquer
Lapis lazuli
Iron
Silk
Tea
Spices
MONGOLIA
Gobi Desert
Great Wall
CENTRAL ASIA
THE SILK ROAD
Kashgar
Xian
Antioch
Tyre
PERSIA
ARABIA
HIMALAYAS
INDIA
CHINA
SOUTHEAST ASIA
COULD GAO BE TRUSTED?
AS WE ARRIVED AT THE PALACE, I WONDERED...
...WAS DUKE SONG RIGHT?
AND IT WAS HIS SHOWING OFF, FLASHING HIS BLADE...
...THAT STARTED THE ATTACK!
ATTEND ME AT COURT TOMORROW!
WHY WAS GAO RUDE TO ME?
FORGET ABOUT GAO...
...HE'S ONLY JEALOUS!
I DIDN'T SEE MUCH OF HIS FANCY SWORDPLAY...
...IN THE FIGHT WITH THE PIRATES!

## Trade into China

Chinese merchants made their fortunes mainly by bringing luxury goods into China. These included precious metals, such as gold, and gemstones, such as jade and lapis lazuli. Horses continued to be brought in from the lands to the west. Dyes, perfumes, and ivory were other important imports.

## Trade out of China

Over the centuries, China's main export was silk, which is why the route from China to Europe was known as the Silk Road. This beautiful material was very popular in Ancient Rome. Chinese ceramics, including fine porcelain, were also highly prized outside China. Other exports included lacquer, tea, spices, and iron.

## The Silk Road

The main Silk Road led from Xian in northern China to Central Asia and then to ports on the Mediterranean Sea. Along the way, goods passed from merchant to merchant; few traders traveled the whole route. The journey could be dangerous as the route crossed deserts and mountains and attacks by thieves were common.

Camels can survive in the harsh desert land that the Silk Road crosses

The groups of camels carrying goods are called caravans

Some caravans are made up of hundreds of camels

Continued from previous page

# City of Splendor

For many centuries, China's cities were the largest and most splendid in the world. They were planned using the ancient practice of *feng shui*, in which objects were placed in harmony with nature. Cities were usually square or rectangular in shape. Unlike many cities elsewhere, they were mainly constructed of wood. This allowed them to be quickly built—but easily destroyed.

**1 City within a City**
The emperor's palace, within its own walled city, is in the north. The imperial family and officials live to the east of it. Traders and others live to the west.

**9 Guarding the Gate**
Each of the city's 12 gates is guarded by a tall watchtower from which guards look for danger. The soldiers live in the gatehouse.

**10 Schoolwork**
At the school, students are studying subjects such as music, agriculture, writing, and geography. They are hoping to pass the civil service entrance exam.

**8 City Walls**
All cities are surrounded by brick and earth walls up to 50 feet (16 meters) thick. The streets are grouped into small areas called wards.

**7 Rich Passenger**
Slaves carry a rich or noble lady through the streets in a sedan chair. Screens shade her from prying eyes and the glare of the sun.

THE NEXT DAY, THE MASTER OF THE ROYAL MUSIC LED ME TO SEE THE EMPEROR.

HURRY UP, BOY!
A BANQUET WAS BEING PREPARED.

STOP STARING!

THE EMPEROR WAS TRYING ON NEW ROBES.

MOST GLORIOUS, MY LORD...

YOUR MAJESTY...
...I HAVE BROUGHT THE BOY!

...EH???
I WONDERED WHO THE GIRL WAS.

THE EMPEROR DISMISSED HIS TAILOR...

IS THE MUSIC FOR THE BANQUET READY?
...AND BECKONED US CLOSER.

YES, SIR.
I, MYSELF, WILL PLAY!

NO, I WANT THE BOY TO PLAY!

2 Fire!
The houses have a wooden frame, mud plaster walls, and tiled roofs. Fires are common as these materials catch light easily.
3 Space for All
Traditionally, large cities have 12 main streets. Each one is wide enough for traffic, market stalls, and even a temporary stage for drama.
4 Well of Heaven
The traditional house for the wealthy is built around a courtyard called the "well of heaven."
5 Courtyard Life
Around the courtyard are sleeping quarters, a hall, women's quarters, a kitchen, storage rooms, and workshops.
6 Selling Goods
Shops sell goods from all over the world, as well as local produce. Umbrellas, a Chinese invention, shade the goods and the shopkeepers from the sun.
THE BOY!??
BUT I, ER... OF COURSE, MY LORD!
HE WILL TAKE THE PLACE OF HONOR BY ME!
I COULDN'T BELIEVE MY LUCK.
BUT LATER, AS I TRIED TO PRACTICE...
CONGRATULATIONS, SHEN!
I HEARD THE EMPEROR WANTS YOU TO PLAY FOR HIM AT THE BANQUET.
YES, BUT I'M DOOMED!
I CAN'T MAKE...
...MUSIC ON A ZITHER LIKE THIS!
REALLY?
THEN MAYBE I CAN HELP YOU.
IT'S YOUR BIG CHANCE TO IMPRESS THE EMPEROR!
Story continues on next page

Continued from previous page

IT'S FOR YOU, SHEN.
I HOPE YOU LIKE IT!
NOT A WORD!
YOU SAVED MY LIFE!
IT'S THE MOST BEAUTIFUL ZITHER I'VE EVER SEEN!
HOW CAN I EVER THANK YOU?
NO NEED. JUST PLAY WELL...
...AT THE BANQUET TOMORROW.
HOW NICE!
EH?
MEILING, AN HONOR!
WHAT A FANTASTIC ZITHER!
Loading the furnace
Iron ore is heated in the furnace
Air is pumped into the furnace to make the temperature hotter
Workers drive the air pump
Supplies of iron ore
Molten iron flows into a clay mold

# Great Inventors

The Chinese were remarkable inventors. Many of their inventions, such as paper-making, magnetic compasses, and gunpowder, changed the world. Other Chinese inventions include printing, wheelbarrows, locks, and keys.

### Star Study

The Chinese believed in astrology—the influence of the planets on human affairs—and closely studied the night sky. They drew up the first map of the stars and were the first to note sunspots, exploding stars, and the passage of comets.

### Navigators

The Ancient Chinese discovered that lodestone, a type of iron ore, could be made to point north. In the first century, they worked out how to make needles point north by magnetizing them and so invented the compass. Compasses were first used to plan the position of cities, but later they became a tool to navigate ships.

### Iron Working

The Chinese were the first to make cast iron. The iron ore was heated in a furnace and then the molten iron was shaped (cast) in a mold. Cast iron was used to make weapons and tools.

Story continues on next page

## Acupuncture

Acupuncture is a form of medicine in which needles are placed into points in the body. The needles are thought to affect the *qi* (energy) that flows through the body along 12 lines called meridians. Acupuncture started in about 2700 BCE. It is still used all over the world.

## Paper-Making

Paper was being made in China in about 100 CE. The invention spread slowly across the world, reaching Europe in the 1100s. Chinese paper was made from silk waste, bark, hemp, or bamboo.

## Gunpowder Weapons

Gunpowder, a mixture of sulfur, charcoal, and saltpeter, was invented in around 850 CE. At first, it was used for fireworks, but by the 10th century, gunpowder weapons had been developed. These included bombs, rockets, and mines. Later, soldiers used gunpowder to fire missiles, such as huge darts, from bamboo tubes.

手厥陰心包經之圖
Assistant with clean needles
Skilled acupuncturist applies needles of different lengths and thickness
Patient in relaxed position
Soaking the bamboo
Cutting bamboo
After soaking the bamboo is boiled to make a mushy pulp
Screen is dipped in pulp
Pulp forms a thin layer of paper on the screen
Finished sheet of paper
Paper is pressed and dried, then peeled off the screen
Fiery dart
Rocket launcher
Firing tube
Missile ready for firing
...AND THE EMPEROR'S JEALOUS LITTLE PET.
YOU'D BETTER WATCH HER, SHEN.
WHO IS SHE?
SHE'S THE DAUGHTER OF THE CAPTAIN OF THE GUARD...
I MUST GO!
PLAY WELL AT THE BANQUET, BOY!
SORRY!
I REALLY AM SO CLUMSY!
IS IT FOR THE BOY?
FROM DUKE SONG, I PRESUME.
HOW VERY...
...THOUGHTFUL!
SNAP!
YOU NEARLY TRAPPED MY FINGERS!

CONTINUED FROM PREVIOUS PAGE

# THE TERRA-COTTA ARMY

Qin Shihuangdi was a proud man who wanted his achievements as a warrior and conqueror to live on after his death. To achieve this, he had a number of huge pits dug next to his tomb near the city of Xianyang. Into these pits, a whole army of life-size clay (terra-cotta) figures was placed. The realistic models of soldiers, horses, and chariots were to guard the emperor in the afterlife.

TOO WORRIED TO SLEEP...
...I WENT OUTSIDE...
...AND STOOD WATCHING THE STARS.
ISN'T THAT...
...COUNT GAO?!

**1 POTTERY SOLDIERS** The figures are made from local clay. They are modeled, fired (to make them go hard), and painted outside the pits in workshops.

**10 DIFFERENT LOOKS** Like a real army, the soldiers all have different faces and expressions. It is even possible to tell what part of China a soldier is from.

**11 BATTLE READY** The troops are positioned as if ready for battle and are holding bronze weapons, including crossbows, bows, spears, swords, and axes.

**9 HATS AND HAIRSTYLES** Officers and chariot drivers wear helmets. Most ordinary soldiers are bare-headed, but their hair is braided and knotted in elaborate styles.

**8 BOTTOM HEAVY** To help it stay upright, the lower body of the soldier is solid but the upper body and head are hollow.

I WONDERED WHERE HE WAS GOING SO LATE.

HE DISAPPEARED OUT OF SIGHT.

I DECIDED TO FOLLOW HIM.

NO ONE WAS AROUND AT THAT TIME OF NIGHT.

OR SO I THOUGHT!

INTRUDER!!
GUARDS!!

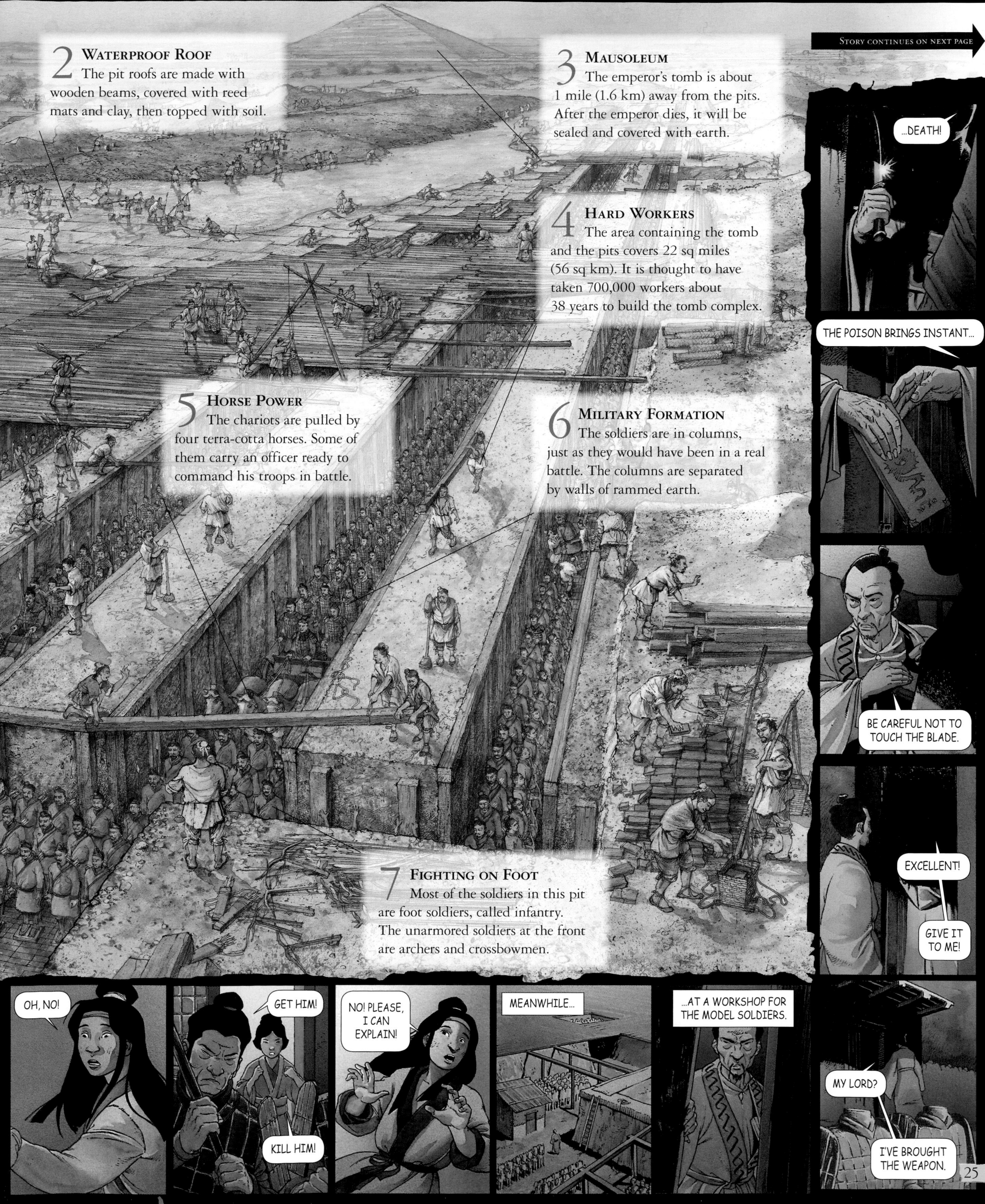

STORY CONTINUES ON NEXT PAGE
2 WATERPROOF ROOF
The pit roofs are made with wooden beams, covered with reed mats and clay, then topped with soil.
3 MAUSOLEUM
The emperor's tomb is about 1 mile (1.6 km) away from the pits. After the emperor dies, it will be sealed and covered with earth.
4 HARD WORKERS
The area containing the tomb and the pits covers 22 sq miles (56 sq km). It is thought to have taken 700,000 workers about 38 years to build the tomb complex.
5 HORSE POWER
The chariots are pulled by four terra-cotta horses. Some of them carry an officer ready to command his troops in battle.
6 MILITARY FORMATION
The soldiers are in columns, just as they would have been in a real battle. The columns are separated by walls of rammed earth.
7 FIGHTING ON FOOT
Most of the soldiers in this pit are foot soldiers, called infantry. The unarmored soldiers at the front are archers and crossbowmen.
...DEATH!
THE POISON BRINGS INSTANT...
BE CAREFUL NOT TO TOUCH THE BLADE.
EXCELLENT!
GIVE IT TO ME!
OH, NO!
GET HIM!
KILL HIM!
NO! PLEASE, I CAN EXPLAIN!
MEANWHILE...
...AT A WORKSHOP FOR THE MODEL SOLDIERS.
MY LORD?
I'VE BROUGHT THE WEAPON.

Continued from previous page

LET ME GO!
THIS PART OF THE PALACE...

WHAT ARE YOU DOING HERE?
...WAS STRICTLY OUT OF BOUNDS.

I COULDN'T SLEEP...
...I GOT LOST!
A LIKELY STORY!

ALL INTRUDERS MUST DIE!

# Dress and Ornament

The Chinese dressed according to their position in society. Emperors wore flowing robes of cotton and silk that made them look bigger and headdresses that added to their height. Members of the court, high-ranking officials, and scholars also dressed in luxurious silk robes. Peasants wore simple clothes of hemp, a type of plant fiber.

## Shoes for Tiny Feet

These silk shoes, no more than 5 inches (13 centimeters) long, were made for a wealthy woman whose feet had been kept unnaturally small. From the age of five or six, a girl's feet were tightly bound in bandages to prevent them from growing normally. This practice began in Song times and continued until it was banned in 1902.

Jade hair ornament

Bird-shaped weights are sewn into long sleeves to stop them from flapping

Golden hairpins from the Tang dynasty

## Splendid Jewels

Both men and women adorned themselves with ornaments made of gold, silver, jade, enamel, and precious stones. These expensive accessories showed a person's position in Chinese society.

Fan for keeping cool

Women make their faces paler with makeup

Finely shaped black eyebrows

## Court Ladies

The emperor's wives lived in their own rooms in the palace. These women are from the 800s, a time before foot binding became fashionable. They enjoyed music and playing with their children and pets. Some wives had great power, such as the Empress Wu Zetian who ruled China from 690 to 705.

NO! I'M INNOCENT!

MEILING! WHAT'S ALL THIS?

FATHER!
I DIDN'T KNOW WHERE I WAS, SIR!

I'M SURE THE BOY MEANT NO HARM.
I DON'T TRUST HIM.

HE PLAYS FOR THE EMPEROR TOMORROW!
RELEASE HIM!

THAT WAS CLOSE!

Story continues on next page

## Soldiers' Uniforms

The Chinese soldiers' uniforms and weapons did not change a great deal over the centuries. Soldiers all wore heavily padded undershirts of wool, cotton, and leather. Their helmets, often with crests, protected the head and neck, but there was never a visor to cover the whole face. The flexible body armor was usually made of small plates of metal riveted together. The most common weapons were swords, spears, and bows. The higher-ranking soldiers, such as officers and generals, wore more elaborate uniforms.

## Women's Clothes

Rich women wore robes, usually of silk, that reached to the ground. The style varied according to fashion. Some robes were made up of a blouse and skirt with a sash tied at the waist, while others were one long garment. Sleeves could be wide or narrow. Men of wealth or status also wore long, flowing robes.

Shang nobleman
Spear
Bow
Sword
Han swordsman
Body armor
Ming general
...HOW DEADLY HIS PLAYING CAN BE!
THE BRAT WILL NEVER KNOW...
THE ZITHER!
Long hair is pinned up to give the appearance of added height
Bronze mirror
In most dynasties, the fashion is for women to have small waists and a slender figure
Young prince playing with pet birds and dog
LATER, I COULDN'T SLEEP.
THOUGHTS KEPT RACING THROUGH MY MIND...
...WHY DID MEILING HATE ME?...
...WHERE WAS GAO GOING?...
...WOULD I PLAY WELL AT THE BAN... ZZZZZZZZZ...

Continued from previous page

THE NEXT DAY...
... I WAS SEARCHED...
...THEN MADE MY WAY NERVOUSLY...
...THROUGH THE COURTIERS...
...TO SIT BEFORE THE EMPEROR!
PLAY, BOY!

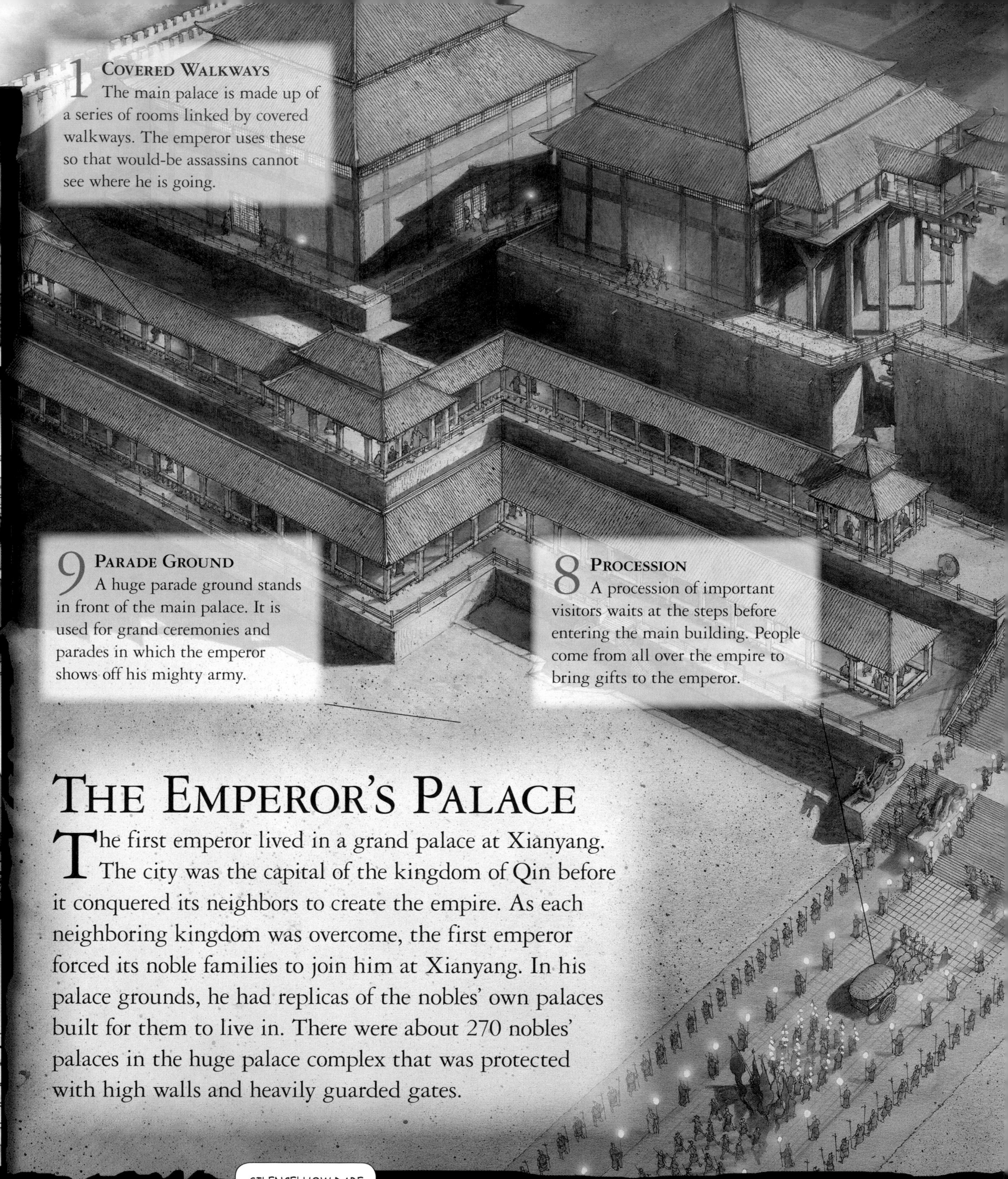

### 1 Covered Walkways

The main palace is made up of a series of rooms linked by covered walkways. The emperor uses these so that would-be assassins cannot see where he is going.

### 9 Parade Ground

A huge parade ground stands in front of the main palace. It is used for grand ceremonies and parades in which the emperor shows off his mighty army.

### 8 Procession

A procession of important visitors waits at the steps before entering the main building. People come from all over the empire to bring gifts to the emperor.

# The Emperor's Palace

The first emperor lived in a grand palace at Xianyang. The city was the capital of the kingdom of Qin before it conquered its neighbors to create the empire. As each neighboring kingdom was overcome, the first emperor forced its noble families to join him at Xianyang. In his palace grounds, he had replicas of the nobles' own palaces built for them to live in. There were about 270 nobles' palaces in the huge palace complex that was protected with high walls and heavily guarded gates.

MY ZITHER! IT SOUNDED...
...TERRIBLE!
HA! WHAT A FOOL!
SILENCE! HOW DARE YOU INSULT ME WITH THIS DIN!
I'LL DEAL WITH YOU AFTER THE CEREMONY!
THE NOBLES BEGAN PAYING HOMAGE TO THE MIGHTY EMPEROR.
GAO FIRST...
...LOOKING AS SINISTER AS EVER.

Story continues on next page

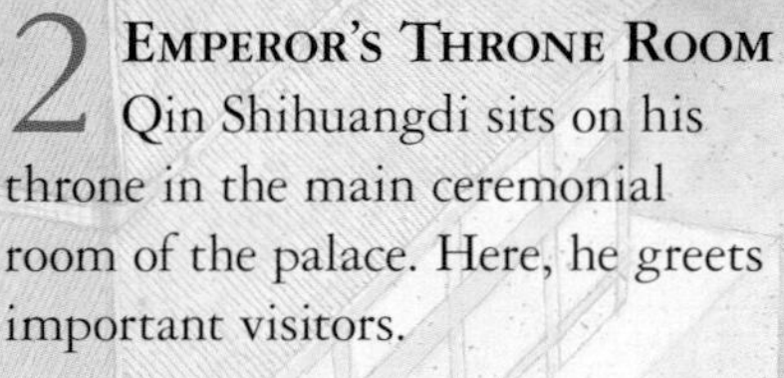

## 2 Emperor's Throne Room

Qin Shihuangdi sits on his throne in the main ceremonial room of the palace. Here, he greets important visitors.

## 3 Pool of Life

A pool of water is an important feature of the throne room. Water represents life and is considered lucky by the Qin.

## 4 Many Pillars

Hundreds of wooden pillars support the palace's many roofs and walls. The interior walls are plastered and painted with frescoes.

## 5 Stairway to Heaven

A giant stairway leads up to the throne room. The emperor is the Son of Heaven and visitors are expected to climb to meet him.

## 6 Mirror Image

The palace is mainly made of wood and built on foundations of rammed earth. Everything is in balance—each side is a mirror image of the side opposite.

## 7 Dragons

Statues of dragons guard the stairway. Qin Shihuangdi is the first emperor to adopt the dragon emblem. The mythical creatures are believed to live in water.

I SUBMIT TO YOUR GREATNESS, O EMPEROR OF THE WORLD!

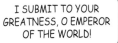

ALL CAME FORWARD, ONE BY ONE...

...INCLUDING MY FRIEND....

...THE KINDLY DUKE SONG.

BUT HIS EASY SMILE...

...SUDDENLY CHANGED!

AND BEFORE I COULD MOVE...

MY LORD!!!
...HE POUNCED!

WHAT...??

NOW I KNEW WHY...
... MY ZITHER HAD SOUNDED SO BAD!

CONTINUED FROM PREVIOUS PAGE

# RELIGIONS AND BELIEFS

Rather than a single religion, China had many faiths and ways of living. From the earliest times, the Chinese prayed to the spirits of their ancestors, and most homes had an altar to dead relatives. Then, during the time of the Warring States (475–221 BCE), the ideas of Daoism and Confucianism, which encouraged peace, became popular. Buddhism arrived later from India.

NOOOOO!!!!
SONG GRABBED THE DEADLY BLADE...

...AND LUNGED FOR THE EMPEROR.

I GRABBED HIS LEGS...

...AND CLUNG ON WITH ALL MY MIGHT!

Laozi on a buffalo traveling around China

Yin yang symbol

## LAOZI AND DAOISM

The Chinese character for "Dao," meaning "the Way" or "the Path."

The founder of Daoism was Laozi (about 604–531 BCE), who may have been a scholar at the Zhou court. He said that happiness came from living a simple life in harmony with nature. Laozi thought that government and laws were unnecessary and didn't believe in duty to the family or the state. In Daoism, all living things share a "life-force" which has two sides, yin and yang. These opposites—yin is dark, cool, and female; yang is light, hot, and male—should be in balance.

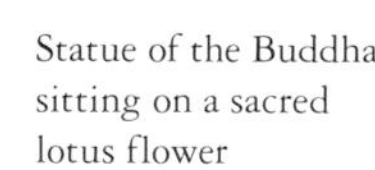

Statue of the Buddha sitting on a sacred lotus flower

## THE BUDDHA

Buddhism was founded by an Indian prince, Siddhartha Gautama (born about 566 BCE). He gave up his family and wealth to seek an end to suffering. When he found the answer, he became the Buddha, which means "awakened one." Buddhists believe that people have many lives, or reincarnations, that only end with *nirvana*, or extinction. To achieve *nirvana*, people must give up wanting things and lead a good life. Monks brought Buddhism to China along the Silk Road in the first century CE. By the Tang dynasty, it was the most popular religion in China.

Shaven-headed Buddhist monk

GET OFF, PEASANT!

BEHIND ME, GAO GRABBED A SWORD...

LET GO, BRAT!

HELP!
I THOUGHT I WOULD DIE!

BUT GAO STRUCK...

Tea
Respectful position
Children serving their parents
Pagoda-style temple
Three to 15 tiers represent many lives on Earth
Bowl for collecting money or food
...AND THE EVIL TRAITOR, MY FRIEND SONG...
ONE SWIFT STROKE...
...LAY DEAD!
SONG!
WAS HE REALLY... AN ASSASSIN?
YES! THE VILLAIN WAS IN THE PAY OF THE CHU.
HOW WRONG I HAD BEEN ABOUT SONG!
GAO, YOU HAVE SERVED ME WELL!
APPROACH, BOY!
I WAS AFRAID THAT I WAS STILL IN TROUBLE.
YOU SEEM TO BRING ME LUCK!
I WANT YOU BY MY SIDE!
BOTH OF YOU!
FRIENDS?
NEVER!

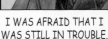

## Confucian Duty

Confucius (551–479 BCE) taught that the path to true happiness lay through obedience to the law, doing one's duty, and respecting the experience of others. This meant that older people, especially parents and grandparents, were greatly honored. In return, the elderly were expected to take care of the young and advise them wisely. In this family scene, children are bowing to their parents and serving them tea.

## Buddhist Temple

Buddhist temples contained a statue or painting of the Buddha and were places of quiet meditation (deep thinking) or chanting. Monks gave up their possessions and led lives of poverty. Ordinary people supported the monks by giving them food, shelter, and clothes. Buddhist temples often included a pagoda—a tower or building with many tiers.

# INDEX